T0000790

National Parks
Olympic

AUDRA WALLACE

Children's Press®
An Imprint of Scholastic Inc.

Content Consultant
James Gramann, PhD
Professor, Department of Recreation, Park and Tourism Sciences
Texas A&M University, College Station, Texas

Library of Congress Cataloging-in-Publication Data
Names: Wallace, Audra.
Title: Olympic / by Audra Wallace.
Description: New York, NY : Children's Press, an imprint of Scholastic Inc., 2018. | Series: A true book | Includes bibliographical references and index.
Identifiers: LCCN 2017025791 | ISBN 9780531235089 (library binding) | ISBN 9780531238110 (pbk.)
Subjects: LCSH: Olympic National Park (Wash.)—Juvenile literature.
Classification: LCC F897.O5 W349 2018 | DDC 979.7/98—dc23
LC record available at https://lccn.loc.gov/2017025791

Printed in Heshan, China 62

Scholastic Inc., 557 Broadway, New York, NY 10012

1 2 3 4 5 6 7 8 9 10 R 27 26 25 24 23 22 21 20 19 18

Front cover (main): Rialto Beach

Front cover (inset): Hikers on a park trail

Back cover: Two bicyclists riding along the Lake Crescent shore

Find the Truth!

Everything you are about to read is true ***except*** for one of the sentences on this page.

Which one is **TRUE**?

T or F Olympic National Park's glaciers have been growing in recent years.

T or F Some trees in the park are more than 200 feet (61 meters) tall.

Find the answers in this book.

Contents

Olympic chipmunk

A field of wildflowers

Bald eagle

Olympic National Park is home to more than 73 miles (117 kilometers) of coastline.

CHAPTER 1

A Long History

The Olympic **Peninsula** in Washington State is often called “a gift from the sea”—and for good reason! From ice-capped mountains and dense rain forests to rushing rivers and rugged shores, there is a lot to explore. This diverse and beautiful area is home to Olympic National Park, one of the most popular parks in the U.S. National Park System. More than three million people visit the park each year.

Born Beneath the Waves

The Olympic Peninsula was formed millions of years ago as lava spewed from volcanoes on the Pacific Ocean floor. Over time, the hardened lava built up to form underwater mountains. Then, about 35 million years ago, two of the huge plates that make up Earth's crust crashed into each other. One of the plates pushed the underwater mountains up above the waves. Today, these mountains are known as the Olympic Mountains.

The Olympic Mountains formed when one piece of Earth's crust moved under another, forcing it upward.

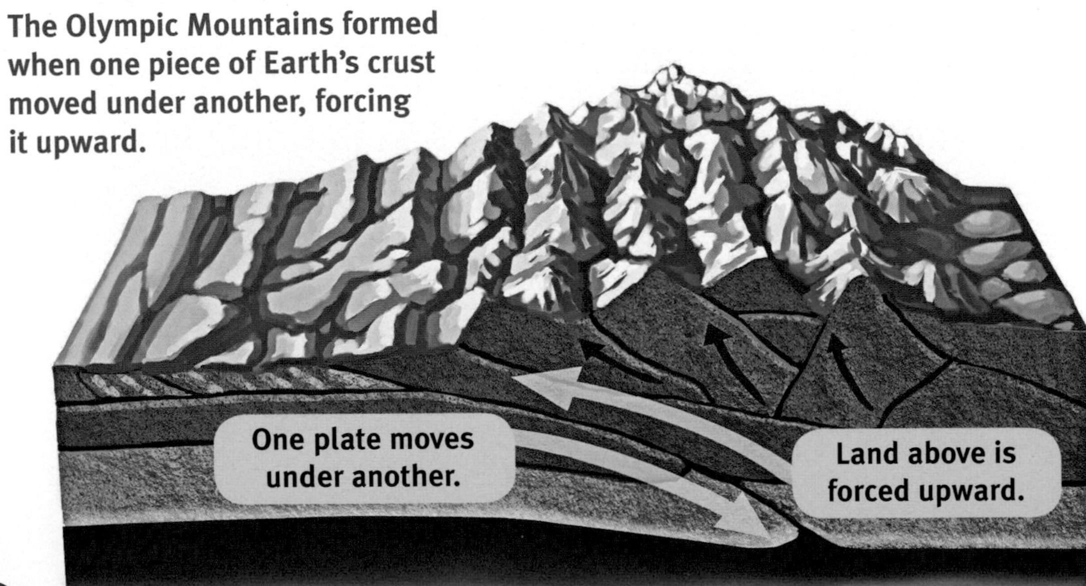

You can still see ancient Makah carvings of whales and people at Wedding Rocks along the coast of the park.

A Land of Many People

People first set foot on the peninsula more than 10,000 years ago. Eight Native American groups eventually settled there. They are the Hoh, Lower Elwha Klallam, Jamestown S'Klallam, Port Gamble S'Klallam, Quileute, Quinault, Skokomish, and Makah. These early peoples hunted the area's many deer and elk. Shellfish, salmon, and marine mammals such as seals and whales were also important sources of food.

Early Explorers

An explorer named Juan de Fuca is believed to be the first European to explore the Olympic Peninsula. In 1592, he claimed the body of water along the peninsula's northern coast for Spain. As a result, this narrow strip of water was named after him. Explorers from other countries, including France and England, soon followed in de Fuca's footsteps.

A Timeline of Olympic National Park

1788

British explorer Captain John Meares names the park's tallest peak, Mount Olympus, after the mythical home of ancient Greek gods.

1850s

Native American groups give up their claim to Olympic Peninsula land in a series of treaties.

1885

Lieutenant Joseph O'Neil leads the first major expedition into the Olympic Mountains.

A Struggle to Survive

The arrival of Europeans had a devastating effect on Olympic's Native American population. Diseases such as smallpox and influenza killed thousands of people. Native Americans also competed with the new settlers for food and land. In the 1850s, the U.S. government forced Olympic's Native Americans onto reservations, or areas of land that was set aside for them, along the shore.

1938

President Franklin D. Roosevelt signs a law creating Olympic National Park.

1958

The number of annual visitors to Olympic National Park reaches one million for the first time.

1977

A farmer discovers the remains of a mastodon, an elephant-like mammal from the Ice Age, just outside of the park.

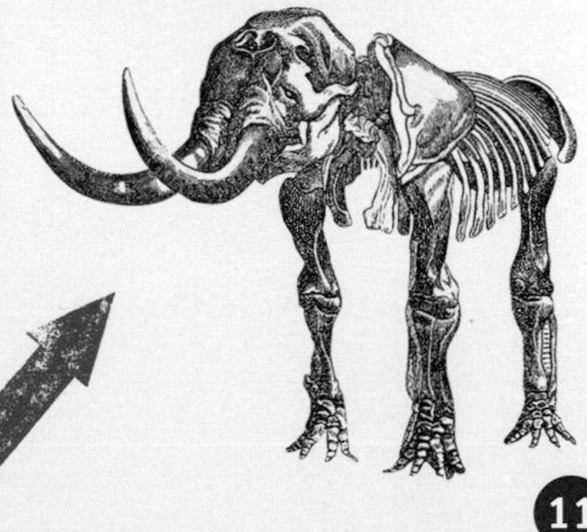

Saving Olympic

President Theodore Roosevelt

By the late 1800s, Olympic's forests had become a hot spot for logging companies and hunters. Trees were cut down for lumber, and elk herds were nearly wiped out. **Conservation** groups encouraged the U.S. government to protect the area. In 1897, President Grover Cleveland set up the Olympic Forest Reserve. This officially protected the plants and animals living there. Twelve years later, President Theodore Roosevelt made Mount Olympus a national monument. Finally, in 1938, President Franklin D. Roosevelt signed a law creating Olympic National Park.

National Park Fact File

A national park is land that is protected by the federal government. It is a place of importance to the United States because of its beauty, history, or value to scientists. The U.S. Congress creates a national park by passing a law. Here are some key facts about Olympic National Park.

Olympic National Park	
Location	Washington State
Year established	1938
Size	922,651 acres (373,384 hectares)
Average number of visitors each year	More than 3 million
Tallest mountain	Mount Olympus at 7,980 feet (2,432 m)
Deepest lake	Lake Crescent at 624 feet (190 m)

Hikers who reach Olympic's mountaintops are rewarded with an incredible view.

CHAPTER 2

Mighty Mountains and More

Giant jagged mountains rise into the clouds above Olympic. The tallest of them is Mount Olympus, at a height of 7,980 feet (2,432 m). Glaciers cover some of the mountains. These thick sheets of ice formed millions of years ago during the Ice Age. Today, there are 60 named glaciers in the park. The most famous is Blue Glacier, which is more than 2.6 miles (4.2 km) long.

The amount of ice that makes up Blue Glacier is equal to about 20 trillion ice cubes.

Visitors who plan to travel along Hurricane Ridge should check the weather and wind speeds before going.

Hair-Raising Hikes

Harsh weather and icy ground make it very dangerous and difficult to climb Olympic's highest mountains. Most of the park's visitors walk or ski along the trail to Hurricane Ridge instead. This spot offers breathtaking views of the park's mountains. But if you want to check out this area, beware: It is named Hurricane Ridge for the powerful winds that blow across it. They can reach speeds of up to 75 miles per hour (121 kilometers per hour)!

Rock Stars

In some spots along Olympic's shores, tall towers of rock stick up from the sand. These formations are called sea stacks. Some are more than 40 feet (12 m) tall. Over time, wind and waves have carved the sea stacks into a variety of fascinating shapes. Some sea stacks even have trees growing on top of them!

A wooden bridge is located above Sol Duc Falls, providing visitors with a stunning view of the water.

Go With the Flow

More than 4,000 miles (6,437 km) of rivers and streams make their way down the sides of the Olympic Mountains. Some of these waterways spill over rocky cliffs as waterfalls. The park's most popular waterfall is Sol Duc Falls. It flows into hot springs, which are pools of water that are heated by underground **magma**. The hot springs are like big, warm baths. Park visitors soak in them to relax.

Lots of Lakes

If you enjoy fishing, you'll find plenty of opportunities to cast a line at Olympic. The park is home to 600 lakes, and they are filled with a wide variety of fish. Lake Crescent is the park's deepest lake, at 624 feet (190 m). Its clear blue water is packed with Beardslee and Crescenti cutthroat trout. These freshwater fish are only found in Olympic. They feed on kokanee, a type of sockeye salmon.

Visitors can take boats or kayaks out on Lake Crescent to catch fish.

CHAPTER 3

Wildlife on the Move

Many different animals roam through Olympic National Park, especially in its forests and meadows. Herds of Roosevelt elk graze on ferns, shrubs, and **lichens**. Black-tailed deer can be spotted nibbling on grass. Mountain lions prowl these areas, too. They hide behind shrubs and small trees, hoping to catch an elk or a deer for dinner.

Roosevelt elk are named after Theodore Roosevelt, the 26th U.S. president.

Into the Woods

Spotted owls also call the park's forests home. They peek out from the trees as Douglas squirrels scamper across the ground below. Millions of banana slugs creep along the forest floor. These slimy 6-inch (15-centimeter) creatures gobble up dead leaves and decaying plants. Other forest dwellers include black bears, snowshoe hares, Pacific tree frogs, and rough-skinned newts.

Barred owls such as this one first arrived in Olympic National Park and the surrounding region as recently as the 20th century.

A humpback whale breaches, or jumps from the water.

Ocean Life

Down by the sea, bald eagles soar overhead. They nest in trees along the beaches. Sea otters float on thick beds of kelp, a type of seaweed. Pacific harbor seals snuggle up on small islands, while orcas dive in and out of the waves. Many people go whale-watching on boats in hopes of seeing a humpback or gray whale on the move.

Migrating coho salmon swim against the current.

A River Adventure

During the summer and early fall, coho salmon **migrate** more than 50 miles (80 km) from the Pacific Ocean to the park's Sol Duc River. There the fish spawn, or lay eggs. Along their journey, they can be seen leaping over a set of small waterfalls called the Salmon Cascades. Bull trout, steelhead, and four other salmon species also travel through the park's rivers and streams. Amphibians such as Cope's salamanders and tailed frogs live there, too.

Special Species

A few animals found in Olympic National Park are not found anywhere else in the world. They include the Olympic marmot, a large rodent that burrows underground and is very social with its fellow marmots. Insects such as the Quileute gazelle beetle and Hulbirt's skipper (a type of butterfly) are also found here. Olympic even has its own unique grasshopper species!

An Olympic marmot keeps watch outside its den.

THE BIG TRUTH!

National Parks Field Guide: Olympic

Field guides have helped people identify wildlife and natural objects from birds to rocks for more than 100 years. Guides usually contain details about appearance, common locations, and other basics. Use this field guide to discover six animals you can spot in the park, and learn fascinating facts about each one!

Roosevelt elk

Scientific name: *Cervus elaphus roosevelti*

Habitat: From mountain meadows and forests to lowland rain forests

Diet: Ferns, shrubs, and lichens from the rain forest; meadow grasses

Fact: A male elk can weigh up to 1,100 pounds (500 kilograms).

Olympic marmot

Scientific name: *Marmota olympus*

Habitat: Mountain meadows above 4,000 feet (1,219 m)

Diet: Flowering plants such as lupine and glacier lilies; plant roots

Fact: This housecat-sized mammal lets out a loud whistle to warn other marmots of predators in the area.

Orca

Scientific name: *Orcinus orca*

Habitat: Ocean; often spotted along the west coast of the United States and Canada

Diet: Fish, squid, birds, other marine animals

Fact: This "killer whale" hunts in pods, or groups, of 5 to 30 whales.

Rhinoceros auklet

Scientific name: *Cerorhinca monocerata*

Habitat: Along the coasts and open sea of the northern Pacific Ocean

Diet: Mainly fish

Fact: This seabird is named for the "horn" on the base of its bill.

Sea otter

Scientific name: *Enhydra lutris*

Habitat: Shallow waters along the northern Pacific coast

Diet: Fish, crabs, sea urchins, clams, abalones, mussels, snails

Fact: This marine mammal uses rocks to crack open the shells of the shellfish it eats.

Olympic chipmunk

Scientific name: *Tamias amoenus caurinus*

Habitat: Forests and meadows

Diet: Seeds, nuts, berries, insects

Fact: This small mammal has large cheek pouches where it can store food to be eaten later.

CHAPTER 4

Roaming the Rain Forests

You might be surprised to learn that there are rain forests in Olympic National Park. A rain forest is a forest that gets heavy amounts of rain each year. There are two types of rain forests. Tropical rain forests are found near the **equator**, where it is hot. Temperate rain forests, like those in Olympic, are found in cooler regions.

More than 100 inches (254 cm) of rain falls in Olympic's rain forests each year.

Layers of the Temperate Rain Forest

In the western area of the park lies the Hoh Rain Forest. There, some of the trees are more than 200 feet (61 m) tall. They include western hemlock and Douglas fir. Sitka spruces also grow here. The trunks of these trees can measure up to 60 feet (18 m) around. In the shadier areas beneath these towering treetops are vine maple, sword fern, and vanilla leaf. Far below is the forest floor. The dense collection of vines, ferns, and leaves above keeps most of the sunlight from reaching the floor. It is dark and damp, and mosses and fungi, such as mushrooms, grow here.

The Hoh Rain Forest was once part of a huge rain forest region that stretched from Alaska to California.

Canopy

This is the top layer of treetops, which receives the most sunlight.

Western hemlock

Sitka spruce

Understory

Shade-loving plants flourish here, where the treetops of the canopy block some of the sun.

Vine maple

Sword fern

Forest Floor

Mosses and fungi flourish in the dark dampness of the rain forest's bottom layer.

Zeller's Bolete mushroom

Liverwort

Plenty of Plants

In all, more than 1,100 plant species grow in Olympic National Park. In **alpine** regions, wildflowers such as pink Douglasia and red willow-herb peek out from rocky ledges. They survive strong mountain winds by growing low to the ground. Avalanche lilies, violets, and starflowers can be found farther down the mountains. Common shrubs in the park include blueberry, juniper, and rhododendron.

White avalanche lilies bloom in the mountains of Olympic National Park.

Tree of Life

Native Americans once depended on forests for everything from food and medicine to shelter and transportation. They called the western red cedar the "tree of life." Native people built longhouses and canoes from this tree's rot-resistant wood. Some even carved giant totem poles out of red cedar. These painted sculptures often honored a family's ancestors or symbolized an ancient legend.

This western red cedar, located in the park, is the world's largest of its kind.

Workers record the park's sounds. This helps them track how much human noise occurs in the area.

CHAPTER 5

The Future of the Park

The National Park Service (NPS) is responsible for conserving Olympic's wild landscape. But one of the biggest threats to the park is out of the NPS's control. Over the past 40 years, Earth's temperature has been rising at a faster pace than usual. Most scientists think that the use of fuels such as coal and oil is to blame. When these fuels are burned, they release gases that trap heat in Earth's **atmosphere**. This has led to a warming of the planet's climate.

A Warming World

Rising temperatures affect Olympic in a big way. Much of the **precipitation** that once fell as snow is now falling as rain. Glaciers need snow to maintain their size. But some have begun to shrink. Others have disappeared completely. During the park's dry summer months, its rivers depend on glaciers for fresh water. Without them, the rivers could run dry and the animals that rely on them—or live in them—will be at risk of dying out.

The glaciers on Mount Olympus and elsewhere are smaller than they were decades ago.

An ancient tree clings to the soil around slowly eroding earth at Kalaloch Creek.

On Shaky Ground

Erosion is another constant challenge for Olympic National Park. Strong winds and waves wear down the park's mountains and rocky coastlines. Park rangers must keep an eye out for loose rocks and tilting trees, especially after a heavy rainfall. Dangerous rockfalls and landslides are common in and around the park.

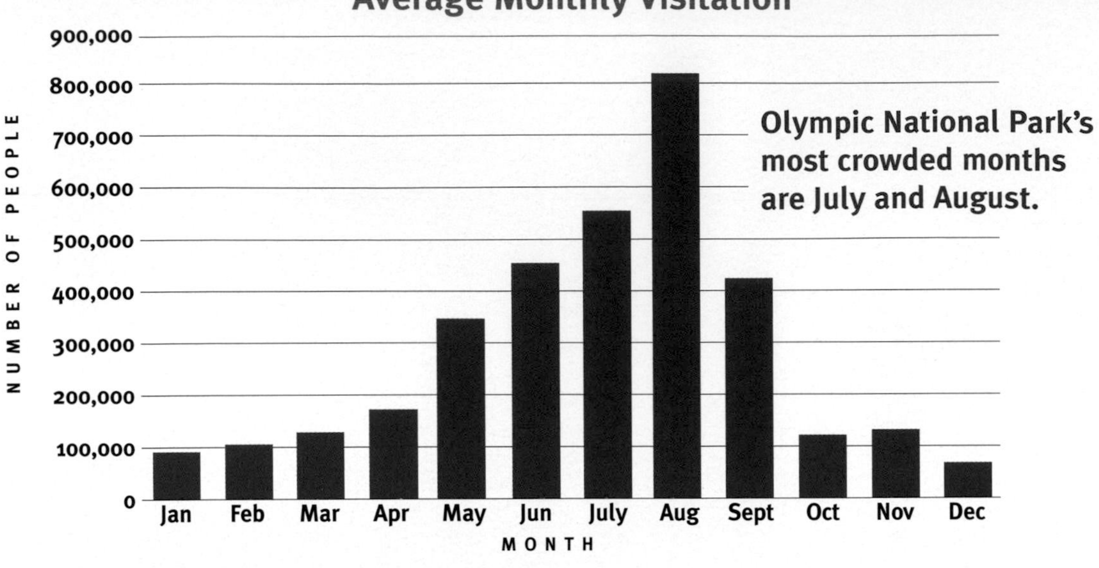

Many Kinds of Visitors

Olympic's native plants and animals have a lot of visitors to contend with, from destructive plants to crowds of humans. Each year, the NPS spends millions of dollars to control **invasive species** in Olympic. Plants such as Scot's broom and Japanese knotweed compete with native plants for sunlight and water. Park rangers must pull, cut, or spray these weeds with chemicals to prevent them from taking over. Rangers also work to keep invasive animals such as wood-boring beetles and zebra mussels out of the park.

The number of people visiting Olympic is on the rise. This makes keeping it clean a tough task. During the summer, people flock to the park to camp, fish, and hike. But they also leave behind a lot of trash. The park provides recycling bins and encourages people to reduce the amount of waste they bring on their trip. By helping to keep the park clean, visitors can play an important role in preserving its natural beauty for years to come. ★

If people are careful and responsible, Olympic National Park will remain a beautiful sight for many years to come.

Map Mystery

About 300 years ago, a mudslide buried a Makah village. A hiker discovered this buried settlement in 1970. More than 55,000 objects from the past were found there. Along what body of water was the village located? Follow the directions below to find the answer.

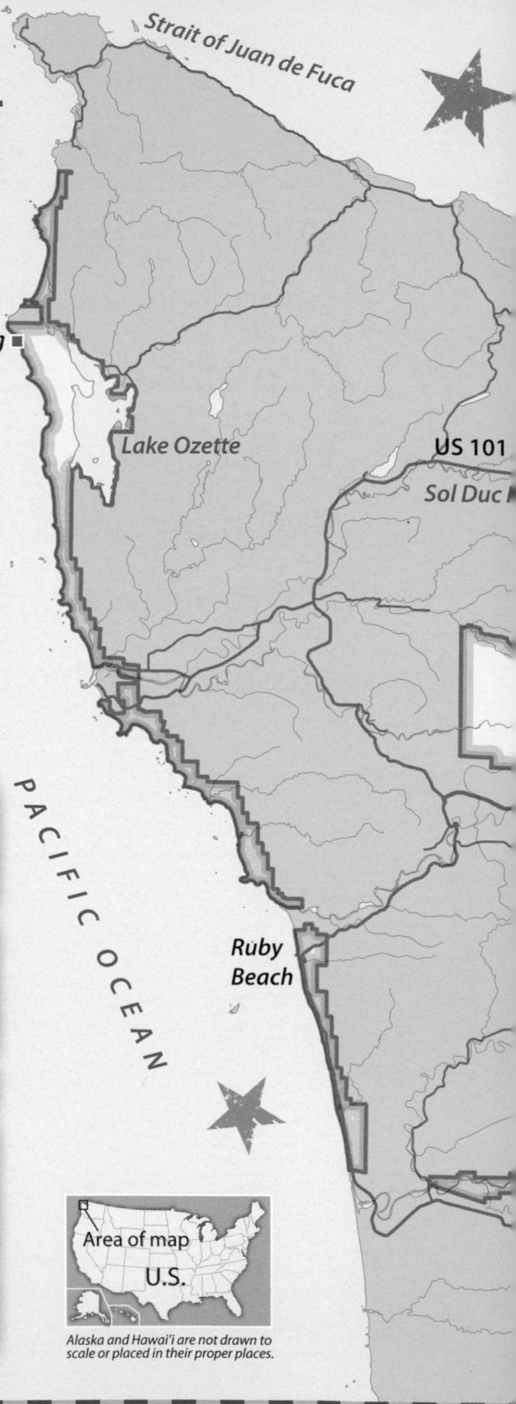

Strait of Juan de Fuca
Wedding Rocks
Lake Ozette
US 101
Sol Duc
PACIFIC OCEAN
Ruby Beach
Area of map
U.S.
Alaska and Hawai'i are not drawn to scale or placed in their proper places.

Directions

1. Start at the park's tallest peak.
2. Hike northwest to the pools of water heated by magma.
3. Travel south to a nearby rain forest.
4. You're almost there! Head west to the beach named after red gemstones.
5. Go north along the coast, then look east to see the banks of this lake.

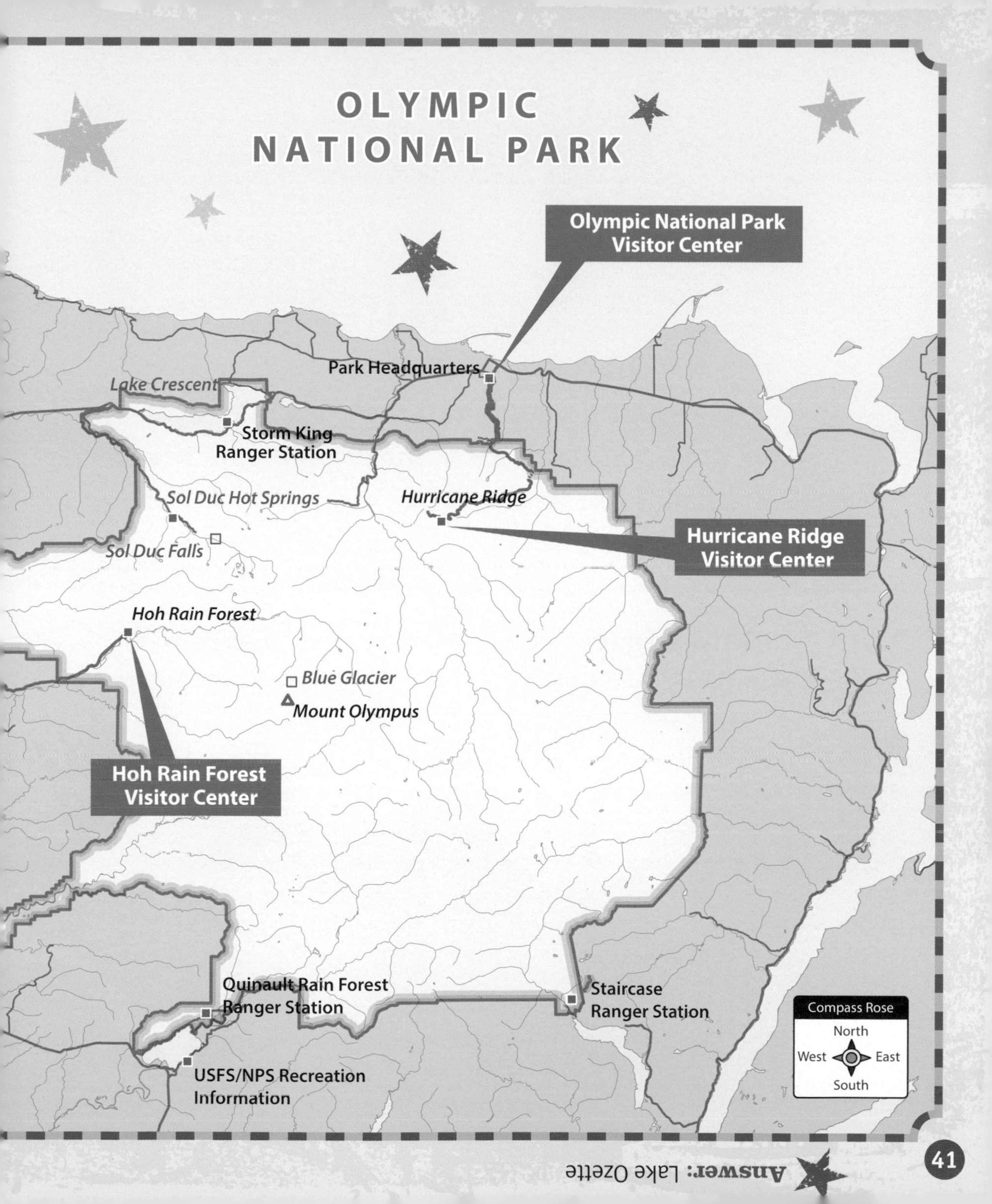

Answer: Lake Ozette

Be an Animal Tracker!

If you're ever in Olympic National Park, keep an eye out for these animal tracks. They'll help you know which animals are in the area.

Bald eagle

Foot length: 6 inches (15 cm)

Beaver

Hind foot length: 6 to 7 inches (15 to 18 cm)

Black-tailed deer
Hoof length: 3.5 inches (9 cm)
Mountain lion
Paw length: 2 to 4 inches (5 to 10 cm)
Olympic black bear
Front paw length: 2 to 5 inches (5 to 12.5 cm)
Snowshoe hare
Paw length: 4 to 5.5 inches (10 to 14 cm)

True Statistics

Number of years since Olympic Peninsula formed: About 35 million

Number of visitors in 2016: 3,390,221

Number of archaeological sites: 650

Number of major rivers: 13

Total distance covered by trails in the park: 611 miles (983.3 km)

Number of named glaciers: 60

Biggest glacier: Blue Glacier at almost 2 square miles (5.2 sq km)

Annual rainfall along the coast and western-facing valleys: Up to 170 inches (431.8 cm)

Annual snowfall on Mount Olympus: 50 to 70 feet (15.2 to 21.3 m)

Did you find the truth?

F Olympic National Park's glaciers have been growing in recent years.

T Some trees in the park are more than 200 feet (61 meters) tall.

Resources

Books

Benoit, Peter. *Temperate Forests*. New York: Children's Press, 2011.

Flynn, Sarah Wassner, and Julie Beer. *National Parks Guide U.S.A.* Washington, DC: National Geographic, 2016.

Stein, R. Conrad. *Washington*. New York: Children's Press, 2015.

Visit this Scholastic website for more information on Olympic National Park:

★ www.factsfornow.scholastic.com
Enter the keyword **Olympic**

Important Words

alpine (AL-pine) having to do with mountains

atmosphere (AT-muhs-feer) the mixture of gases that surrounds a planet

conservation (kahn-sur-VAY-shuhn) the protection of valuable resources, especially wildlife and plants

equator (ih-KWAY-tur) an imaginary line around the middle of Earth that is an equal distance from the North and South Poles

invasive species (in-VAY-siv SPEE-sheez) an animal or plant that moves into an area and alters or harms the plants or animals that are found there

lichens (LYE-kuhnz) flat, spongelike growth that consists of algae and fungi growing close together

magma (MAG-muh) melted rock found beneath Earth's surface

migrate (MYE-grate) to move to another area or climate at a particular time of year

peninsula (puh-NIN-suh-luh) a piece of land that sticks out from a larger landmass and is almost completely surrounded by water

precipitation (pri-sip-ih-TAY-shuhn) the falling of water from the sky in the form of rain, sleet, hail, or snow

Index

Page numbers in **bold** indicate illustrations.

About the Author

Audra Wallace graduated from Ithaca College, where she studied film production and elementary education. Her passion for writing nonfiction and teaching kids led her to a position with Scholastic. Since 2006, Wallace has written and edited the award-winning classroom magazine *Scholastic News* Edition 3. She and her family enjoy exploring the great outdoors near their home in New York—and beyond!

PHOTOGRAPHS ©: cover main: Konrad Wothe/Minden Pictures; cover inset: Jordan Siemens/Getty Images; back cover: Jordan Siemens/Getty Images; 3: MINT Images/Art Wolfe/Aurora Photos; 4: Danita Delimont/Getty Images; 5 top: Floris van Breugel/NPL/Minden Pictures; 5 bottom: Barbara Helgason/Dreamstime; 6: Nick Hall/Aurora Photos; 8: Spencer Sutton/Science Source; 9: Paul Christian Gordon/Alamy Images; 10: Paul Fearn/Alamy Images; 11 left: GL Archive/Alamy Images; 11 center: Paul Zahl/Natiol Geographic/Getty Images; 11 right: Grafissimo/iStockphoto; 12: PARIS PIERCE/Alamy Images; 13: TMI/Alamy Images; 14: Design Pics Inc/Alamy Images; 16: Jordan Siemens/Getty Images; 17: Education Images/Getty Images; 18: Ethan Welty/Aurora Photos; 19: Nick Hall/Aurora Photos/Alamy Images; 20: John Mahan/Getty Images; 22: MINT Images/Art Wolfe/Aurora Photos; 23: Alexander Safonov/Getty Images; 24: Thomas & Pat Leeson/Science Source; 25: Greg Vaughn/Alamy Images; 26 -27 background: Zamada/Shutterstock; 26 left: JackVandenHeuvel/iStockphoto; 26 right: Gerrit Vyn/NPL/Minden Pictures; 27 top left: Mikhail Akkuratov/iStockphoto; 27 top right: Glenn Bartley/All Canada Photos/Superstock, Inc.; 27 bottom left: Chase Dekker Wild-Life Images/Getty Images; 27 bottom right: Danita Delimont/Getty Images; 28: Woods Wheatcroft/Aurora Photos; 30: Nate Derrick/Shutterstock; 31 top right: Chris Cheadle/Alamy Images; 31 top left: Rex Ziak/Getty Images; 31 center left: Janis Burger/National Park Service; 31 center right: Dominique Braud/Animals Animals/Earth Scenes/National Geographic Creative; 31 bottom left: Tim Zurowski/Shutterstock; 31 bottom right: NNehring/iStockphoto; 31 background: 2009fotofriends/Shutterstock; 32: Floris van Breugel/NPL/Minden Pictures; 33: Konrad Wothe/Minden Pictures; 34: National Park Service/AP Images; 36: Amit Basu Photography/Getty Images; 37: dawgfan1/iStockphoto; 39: YinYang/Getty Images; 42 left: Barbara Helgason/Dreamstime; 42 right: Musat/iStockphoto; 42 eagle track: lenjoyeverytime/Shutterstock; 42-43 animal tracks: Natarto76/Shutterstock; 43 top left: Steven Kazlowski/Superstock, Inc.; 43 top right foreground: GlobalP/iStockphoto; 43 bottom left: Martin Ruegner/age fotostock; 43 bottom right: Tom Reichner/Shutterstock; 43 top right background: Jordan Siemens/Getty Images; 44: Chris Cheadle/Alamy Images.

Maps by Bob Italiano.